WRITE EVERY DAY

MOTIVATE YOURSELF TO SUCCESS IN 10 EASY STEPS

HELENA HALME

CONTENTS

1
INTRODUCTION

Many writing gurus and successful authors talk about how important it is to write every day. But why is it so important? Should every writer do it? I certainly think so. But let me explain why.

Why write every day?

If you want to be a writer, to make writing your profession, writing *something* every day is essential. It is, after all what a writer does. He or she writes. I assume since you are here, you are a writer or have the ambition to be a writer. Whether you want to write a journal, a blog, an autobiography, a novel, or a nonfiction title, you need to commit to putting down some words at some point. Writing every day makes the process of achieving the desired word count easier.

Writing every day means that you can publish more books in less time, which will make it easier for you to make a living out of your writing. I will talk about the money side of writing in the next chapter.

Writing is a craft, just like, say, woodworking. The more you practise the craft, the better at it you will become. When you commit to writing every day, you will notice that your writing becomes faster, easier and more polished. (Well, up to a point.)

Writing every day will also feed your creativity. We often believe that creativity is a well that is finite: if we dip into it too often, it will run out. In my experience, the exact opposite is true: the more we write, the more infinite the well is. There are limitations to this theory, of course. Like everything in life, you mustn't overdo it. In Chapter 10, I talk about how you also need to take care of yourself to guard against burnout.

In this book, I will go into detail about why writing every day makes you a better writer, but I will also cover the difficulties authors face, such as the dreaded writer's block, and how to overcome them. Furthermore, I will show you tips and tricks on how to motivate yourself to write every day. I will also tell you how my writing career (eventually) led me to a daily writing routine, and with that to publishing success.

Become a writer

If you wish to make your career as a writer, you need to sell enough books to support your lifestyle. It's well known that if a reader falls in love with a book, they want to read more of the author's work. Without being a mathematician, or a marketing guru, it's clear that the more (good) books you publish, the more sales you get each day.

I found this to be true when I began my blog series back in 2009 and published my first novel in 2012. I just wish I'd taken heed of the 'Write Every Day' ethos back then and produced the subsequent novels a lot sooner than I did! This is the reason I want to share my own experiences, including the mistakes, of establishing a sustainable writing routine that leads to success. Writing every day enables you to produce books as quickly as possible.

That's it.

That's the long and short of it.

It's ultimately your decision. Do you want to be a successful writer?

My story

I began taking writing seriously when I enrolled on an MA in Creative Writing at Bath Spa University. After my elation at being accepted on the course, I realized that I would now have to start writing regularly. *Go figure!* I had already completed a novel, but it had taken me years. Fair enough, I had young children at home, as well as a full-time job, so writing time came at a premium.

My writing routine consisted of bursts of activity. I might have a run of two or three weeks when I'd write more or less regularly. Alternatively, I'd write every day for a week or so. But this method had its pitfalls: every time I'd sit at my desk in front of my computer, I'd have to reread almost the entire manuscript, just to get into the story again. And then I'd begin editing instead of writing. Of course, editing is also writing, but when you are in the first draft stage, this can be a killer to both your productivity and creativity. If you had allocated, say, two hours to writing new text, editing what you've already written can swallow up the whole of that time. At this stage, reading and editing can also crush your creativity. I'm not saying that your first draft is never brilliant, but it is a first draft, something you will go back to and modify later. Seeing your 'mistakes' from previous writing sessions before you start a new one can be depressing and make you question whether you can write.

I will go deeper into my techniques for getting fresh, new words down every day later on in this book. But first, let's go back to my own experience. I didn't learn the magic of writing every day until many, many years after the exciting, roller-coaster of my MSCW course.

Coffee and Vodka

No, this is not a story about a particularly lovely cocktail that got me writing every day.

During the year-long MA course, I wrote one novel, COFFEE AND VODKA, which took another six months to edit. In those days, the wonder of self-publishing hadn't taken off (this was in 2005), so I began to explore literary agents. I'd send a few letters and samples of my manuscript off each week. And each week, I'd get a bunch of rejection letters. This wasn't particularly conducive or motiving to starting another novel, but start one I did.

The literary agent

The second book was amazingly easy to write, even though I wrote only at weekends and in the evenings. This novel, *The Red King of Helsinki*, is a spy thriller, a genre I hadn't imagined I'd ever choose. In spite of this, I finished the manuscript in a matter of months. After my previous efforts, this was amazing to me. I also had more success with agents. I was even called to a meeting in

London with a very esteemed agent. This lady had represented Doris Lessing, so I was thrilled to get some face-to-face time with her. She wanted me to do some rewrites. For the first time in my short author career, I forced myself to write every day.

The knowledge that an agent was eagerly waiting for my work was enough for me to forgo TV, sleep and outings with my family. Long story short, the agent never took me on – she didn't like the rewrite even though I'd followed her advice to the T. Oh, well. The book is a much better piece of work for the rewrite.

And the agent's words of encouragement as I left her office still ring in my ears, 'I'll read your future work even if I have to pay good money to buy the books.'

Blogging

In spite of the literary agent's kind comment, my world crash around me when I received the rejection. I was convinced I'd never be a writer and would never be published. It wasn't until a year or so later, when I started blogging about my own life, that I began writing in earnest again.

In those days, in 2009, blogging was 'the thing', and I soon discovered an active online community – and readership. This community encouraged me to write a chapter of my story, 'How I Came to Be in England', every week. When I moved my blog over to my website in 2012, I'd had half a million hits on the Blogger site. It soon became apparent that, instead of a biography, I was writing a novel. Again, I was writing nearly every day. A few years later, in 2012, I published a rewritten version of these blog posts as *The English Heart*. This novel is still one of my best-selling titles and led to a successful series.

Self-publishing

Because of my previous experience with a literary agent, and because Amazon had by then bought out KDP Publishing, I decided to self-publish the three books I had written. And, boy am I glad I did! On the launch day, *The English Heart* sold more than 500 copies. I hadn't done any marketing for the book, apart from letting my blog followers know that the novel I'd blogged about was coming out. That same day, I'd been asked to speak to a group of writers in

Bath about self-publishing. A friend from my MA course ran a writing group and, knowing I was about to publish my first novel, asked me to come and talk to the group. I was by no means an expert, but in those early days there were very few indie authors, so we were in high demand!

During the evening I kept refreshing the KDP Reports page on my phone. I was amazed by the growing numbers of downloads. Although 500 copies doesn't sound many compared to today's sales figures, to me this was remarkable. I'd never had so many people wanting to read my work. I soon had positive reviews on Amazon, which gave me another massive confidence boost. Publishing my first book was the best motivator I could have. What could be better than writing and publishing your work whenever you want? I went on to write five more books in *The Nordic Heart* series, but I was still not writing regularly, let alone every day.

NaNoWriMo

It wasn't until I took part in NaNoWrMo (National Novel Writing Month) in 2014, that I began a proper writing routine.

NaNoWriMo is a programme that happens every November. Participants undertake to write 50,000 words in a month. I had wanted to take part in this event for several years, but always backed out at the last minute. Finally, in 2014, I achieved my goal with a few days to spare.

In order to write 50,000 words in a month, you have to be disciplined and write every day. They say it takes three weeks to form a habit, and NaNoWriMo certainly worked for me. Now, if I have a day when I haven't written anything, I get a bit jittery. These days I do try to take breaks, but I'm at my happiest if I write every day, be it a blog post, newsletter, or adding words to my current manuscript. Even on holiday, I need to have one or two writing days.

Writing every day

Writing every day has been the route to my success as a creative entrepreneur. I now run a creative business where I divide my time between running a publishing and marketing consultancy and publishing my own books. I produce three to four books a year, and have a five-figure annual income. I am not by any means the most productive of the many indie writers I know, but I believe that by writing a little every day, you can create a sustainable writing business without burning yourself out. I hope I can enthuse you to find your creativity and write every day.

In the next chapter, I'll deal with the reasons why writing every day – or creating a sustainable writing routine – is essential if you wish to become a successful writer.

2

BECOME A BETTER WRITER

Writing is a craft, just like woodworking. The more tables or chairs, or whatever it is you make, the better at it you become.

In the same way, becoming a better writer takes practice, and writing every day is perfect for this. Of course, you probably already do a lot of writing. Perhaps you write lengthy reports or papers, and you almost certainly write daily emails or other messages privately and on social media. So writing every day isn't such a huge leap. However, writing a piece of fiction or nonfiction takes a little more time and concentration. You need to keep at it. And while focusing on details in scenes and chapters, you also need to keep the whole of the story or subject matter in your mind. This is why it's so important to return to your writing project regularly.

When I began writing my first novel, I only managed to get down to looking at the manuscript once or twice a month. Taking long breaks between writing made it difficult to remember what I'd been planning to write next, let alone what the story was. I ended up reading more than writing, and wasting most of the time I'd set aside for writing. I learned that even if I sat down for only an hour each day, and set down just a few words, I had a clear picture of where the story was going before I wrote a single word. The same applies to the nonfiction titles I write. The project and its various parts are much clearer in my mind if I return to the project every day.

Practice makes your writing better. You'll notice how your sentence structure improves and how you are able to write better descriptions and dialogue. Your brain will be more practised at keeping the elements of the story in your head. Naturally, it's important to learn about the craft, and to read a lot of books in your genre, but it's the doing that makes you perfect.

Routine feeds the brain

Writing every day gives you a routine. There's a plethora of famous writers who attribute their success to the routine of writing every day.

WH Auden, the poet, said, 'Routine, in an intelligent man, is a sign of ambition.' (https://medium. com/the-mission/the-daily-routine-of-20-famous-writers-and-how-you-can-use-them-to-succeed-1603f52fbb77) He probably meant 'man' in the sense of human, though being a Victorian, it may be that he didn't think women could be intelligent. But that's by the by. Routine is good for mental health, lowers anxiety, and is good for creativity.

The celebrated contemporary novelist Haruki Murakami says that he keeps to a routine every day without variation. 'The repetition itself becomes the important thing; it's a form of mesmerism. I mesmerize myself to reach a deeper state of mind. But to hold to such repetition for so long – six months to a year – requires a good amount of mental and physical strength. In that sense, writing a long novel is like survival training. Physical strength is as necessary as artistic sensitivity.'(https://jamesclear.com/daily-routines-writers)

Whereas the Russian novelist Leo Tolstoi, author of *War and Peace*, said, 'I must write each day without fail, not so much for the success of the work, as in order not to get out of my routine.' Tolstoi is said to have worked in isolation – no one was allowed to enter his study, and the doors to the adjoining rooms were locked to ensure that he would not be interrupted. (Mayo Oshin for Mission.org)

The prolific thriller writer Stephen King writes six pages every day. He says, 'I have my vitamin pill and my music, sit in the same seat, and the papers are all arranged in the same places... The cumulative purpose of doing these things the same way every day seems to be a way of saying to the mind, you're going to be dreaming soon.' (Mayo Oshin for Mission.org)

My own experiences certainly bear this theory out. I only began writing every day after I took part in the National Novel Writing Month, NaNoWriMo in 2014. Having committed to writing 50,000 words in a month gave me the inspiration I needed to get into a writing routine. Each day, I'd wake at 5.30am, settle at my writing desk at 6am, and write until 9am, when I'd have breakfast. I did this seven days a week. Now, I have eased off a bit and write five mornings a week. If I get on well, I write into the afternoon, but I always make sure that I have at least 1,000 words done before I finish. My goal is 2,000 words a day, and that is what I generally produce, but I try not to stress myself out with an unachievable goal. (I talk more about setting targets in Chapter 5.) Since that first NaNOWriMo year, I've published nine fiction and three nonfiction titles.

Clear vision

The more you write, the clearer your vision on your project (and even on your life!) becomes.

Writing has an incredible ability to reach the deepest recesses of our minds. This is why writing a diary or a journal is often part of a mental health programme. Writing increases mindfulness because it is a form of self-expression. Any creative outlet is generally considered good for our mental health, and writing is a direct expression of our thoughts.

When you write as a profession, having a clear mind, or a vision of your writing goals as part of your life goals, is hugely important.

A coherent understanding of your writing project makes completing it effortless. When you return to that project every day, your idea of what the finished book will look like gets clearer each time, making it easier and easier to add to it. Naturally, there will be days when you feel as though you're in the middle of a thick forest with no way out, and later in this book, I will give you tools to deal with these kinds of days. I promise you, the difficult days will become fewer the more you write.

In the next chapter, I'll show you how writing every day will increase your income as a writer.

3

MONEY IS NOT A DIRTY WORD

Why Write Every Day?

Above, I touched briefly on the reasons why writing every day brings success. A sustainable writing routine fills your creative well, makes you a better writer and can bring you financial prosperity.

Of course, most writers are not merely – or even at all – motivated by money. Still, we all have to eat, right? And if you, like me, want to be a full-time writer, you need to be able to make money from your writing.

The idea that writers should not have to think about matters such as money is hugely outmoded.

In fact, I'd argue that this idea has never really had any base in reality. Writers from Shakespeare and Dickens to Stephen King have always had to consider making a living.

Shakespeare was, by all accounts, an astute businessman, investing in property and a theatre company (Prospectmagazine.co.uk).

Dickens' writing was influenced by the sudden poverty he was plunged into at the age of twelve, when his father got into financial difficulty. The change in circumstances gave him what biographer Michael Slater describes as a 'deep personal and social outrage'. For example, he began writing *A Christmas Carol* when he was 'in debt up to his eyeballs' (*New York Post,* 9 December 2017) and realized that the Christmas holiday was a popular theme. Dickens might never have written his plea for charity if he hadn't been desperate to make money (there's some irony there). As a pioneer, he also published the story himself, mainly to make more money, but also to have artistic control over the production. *A Christmas Carol* has never been out of print and the story has been adapted for film, TV and theatre. In our family, no Christmas is complete without several viewings of *The Muppet Christmas Carol*.

More books = more sales

So, it's important to consider money when thinking about writing as a career. As I mentioned in the introduction, the more books you publish, the more you'll earn, but there is a caveat. The books have to be good, or even excellent. *A Christmas Carol* is a masterpiece, even if it was born out of financial need. I know we can't in our wildest dreams believe we'll be the next Dickens, but it's useful to remember that even the masters of the craft wrote some of their best work under financial pressures. Your next book doesn't have to be a classic that will be read for hundreds of years to come (although you never know if you don't write it!), but it still needs to be the very best work you can produce. Pushing out below-par work will not automatically bring success. But the more you write, the better you will become. So, for now, all you need to concentrate on is how to set up a sustainable writing routine that ensures you produce a certain number of words a day.

An example

Let's consider the example of an author who has written and published four books. These books can be standalone, or in a series, it doesn't matter. The books are published three months apart. I've made the following assumptions:

1. A new author publishes four books three months apart
2. Example shows twelve-month royalty income
3. Books are priced between $0.99 and $2.99, giving an average royalty rate of $1.58
4. Each new release forms a spike and increases backlist sales (sale-through)
5. No costs for editing, proofreading, cover design or any other services are included

With these assumptions, income in the first eight months will look something like this:

	Book 1	Book 2	Book 3	Book 4	TOTAL	SALES
Month 1	50				50 £	79.13
Month 2	40				40 $	63.30
Month 3	60	70			130 $	205.73
Month 4	50	60			110 $	174.08
Month 5	40	50			90 $	142.43
Month 6	50	60	90		200 $	316.50
Month 7	40	50	80		170 $	269.03
Month 8	30	40	70		140 $	221.55
Month 9	40	50	80	110	280 $	443.10
Month 10	30	40	70	100	240 $	379.80
Month 11	20	30	60	90	200 $	316.50
Month 12	10	20	50	80	160 $	253.20
TOTAL						$ 2,864.33

Royalties for 4 titles published at 3-month intervals

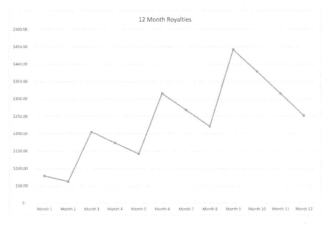

Chart view of the above figures

It's fairly easy to see that each new book will bring more sales, and the aggregate result of giving readers something else to buy or download will produce a steady income. Just think, if this imaginary writer published another four books a year for another ten years! As long as the author keeps marketing all his books, the backlist alone will bring a steady income, especially if he or she pushes out new titles on a regular basis.

The figures above invented by me are informed by ten years of experience. My intention is to show that if you keep producing books, your readership, your book sales, and ultimately your income, will grow.

In the next chapter I'll talk more about the reason why you may not be writing, and how to find out why.

4
WHY AREN'T YOU WRITING?

It's worth repeating that writing is your most important job. If you want to be a successful writer, you have to write. Nothing else matters. So why, then, aren't you writing?

Since you are reading this book, you must struggle with the process, but have you ever asked yourself the actual question? Why didn't I write today, yesterday, this week, month? What is really stopping you from sitting down and working on your manuscript? I think it's worth examining the real reasons why we don't write (when we know we should) before we go any further with my tips and tricks for writing every day.

Free writing

In order to get an answer to this question, I would recommend sitting down and writing, by hand, if possible, your thoughts on why you are not doing what you want to do, ie write.

Orna Ross, writer, poet and the founder of the Alliance of Independent Authors, advocates in her *Go Creative* series of books using something called F-R-E-E-Writing.

'F-R-E-E stands for writing Fast, Raw and Exact-But-Easy' (Orna Ross https://www.ornaross.com/f-r-e-e-writing/)

You can go to Orna's website and look up the tutorial, but the technique basically entails writing out a problem that you have. You take a notebook and a pen and start writing whatever comes to mind. Don't think, just write. You can set a time limit, say one or two minutes, and write continuously as fast as you can. With this type of exercise, you can reach your deeper feelings and find answers to problems. You can ask your brain a question and let your hands find the answer without consciously thinking about it. It works for me and many other creatives. It may not work for you, but if you don't know why you aren't writing, I'd recommend starting with F-R-E-E-Writing. It may provide you with an answer.

You can also use meditation, mindfulness, or just a good old-fashioned walk in the woods to examine your lack of motivation. Do whatever works for you.

Whatever technique you use, you may be surprised by what you find. There are several common reasons why writers don't write, but it often boils down to a deep-seated lack of confidence. Whatever its manifestation – thinking we are too busy, not having the headspace to write, not knowing what to write, lacking inspiration, or not being able to decide which project to choose – it often boils down to doubt. Will what I write be good enough?

You're not alone. I'd wager that at some point in their career, every writer feels this way. Many writers feel this way *all the time*, but they carry on because they want to be writers. They push through the blocks that the little voice of their fearful subconscious sets for them and write anyway.

Remember when you are examining the reason for your lack of motivation or commitment to writing, fear of failure is very, very common.

Mindset

Once you've found out why you are not writing, make sure you deal with it. Consider your inability to write as a business problem that you need to solve. Take away – if you can – the emotional side of the issue and just consider practically what you can do to make writing every day easier. In the following chapters I go through practical ways to make it easier to write every day.

If, however, you think you are not writing because of a lack of confidence, read on.

As I said, the reason writers aren't writing often stems from uncertainty and negative thinking. I struggle with this damaging fear all the time. But I keep reminding myself that my previous books have been much loved by readers. I also remind myself that draft is just that, a draft. There will be many more drafts, many corrections, and rewrites, some of which I will make myself and some of which my professional editor will suggest for me. But I cannot correct, rewrite or edit a black page.

But I still suffer from this lack of confidence, and have to battle my internal demons every day. My particular issue is that I think of writing as a luxury and I need to complete all sorts of unpleasant tasks, like doing my bookkeeping, before I can settle down to adding words to the current manuscript. It's taken me years to convince myself that writing is not a reward. Neither is it a punishment. It's my job. I needed to change my mindset to writing, something I discovered through taking part in NaNoWriMo. Suddenly an outside force told me that I had to complete a certain number of words each day. Miraculously, I managed it.

Your journey to changing your mindset could look very different from mine. Accepting that you need to change the way you view your writing is the first step. Perhaps you also need to convince your nearest and dearest of your commitment to being a writer. Perhaps they have not been supportive, because they have seen that you are not serious about your writing. Something like taking part in NaNoWriMo could convince them, as well as you, that you really want to be a writer. Of course, you can also do this off your own back, any month of the year. Set a target of thirty days during which you will write 50,000 words (just short of a novel) and tell everyone about it. This will give you accountability and will earn you the respect of those who may have been doubting you. Most importantly, it will show *you* that you *can* write every day and reach a goal.

Confidence

As I've already mentioned, gaining confidence is the key to getting yourself into a writing routine that will bring success. But how to do it if you are just starting out and nobody believes you can become a writer? Perhaps you've had a few unsuccessful rounds with literary agents, trying to get your book accepted by a publisher. Perhaps you have a pile of refusal letters buried deep inside your drawer or stored in a file on your email server. (Believe me, I have a veritable forest of 'No, thank you' replies from the days when you got actual letters from agents and publishers.)

Perhaps you have had a few books published, either independently or traditionally, but they are not doing as well as you hoped?

In both cases, ask yourself what it is that *you* want. Getting a literary agent and a publishing deal has never been more difficult than it is today. In most cases, a refusal has nothing to do with the quality of the writing. It's everything to do with what the agent thinks they can sell, what their current list looks like, and what they consider fashionable. Most importantly, it is one person's point of view. Agents and publishers are old-fashioned gatekeepers in the industry, and I believe the agents' days (at least) are numbered.

But that's another discussion.

If you have a few books out, and they are not selling, it may be difficult to find the confidence to keep writing. Believe me, I've been here too.

However, there could be a multitude of reasons why your current list isn't selling. Most of the reasons will be to do with marketing: the cover, the blurb, the genre, the metadata, the sales channel, or the lack of successful advertising. These are just a few of the possible reasons. Did you notice that I didn't even mention the writing?

At some point you need to deal with these reasons. There is a lot of online help available. But, and this is a big but, if you want to carry on as a writer, the best way to get your backlist moving is to write another book. Make it better than your previous titles and you may have a best seller on your hands. You can see from the charts in Chapter 2 how a new book lifts the sales of the previous books.

Many readers binge on an author's work once they find a story they love. The books don't need to be in a series, although it is much easier to get so-called read-throughs if they are. As long as your books are similar, in the same genre (although even this isn't always necessary), readers will find your backlist.

If you are just starting out, the world is literally your oyster. Write, write and write, and don't worry about who believes in you and who doesn't.

The only thing that matters is what you want to do.

Fear

To get the confidence to write every day, you need to deal with the fear that we all have inside us. The little voice that tells us that we will never succeed sits inside every writer, I guarantee. It tells us that no one will ever want to read the books we produce and we will never become best-selling writers.

We need to face this fear head on.

What if no one ever wants to read the book I'm writing? This will not be the case if you have done your homework and use professionals to help you edit and proofread your manuscript and produce a good cover, but let's say you get only a handful of reads and reviews. What do you do? You dust yourself off and write another book. That one will be better than the last (they always are; remember writing is a craft and you improve the more you do it).

What if I never succeed?

Ask yourself what success looks like. Be realistic. If you want to make enough money to live on, calculate how much you need, and then look at how many books per month, per year, you need to sell in order to make this come true. Then look at how many books this will take, and how many you can write in a year.

Say you want to earn $50,000 a year. For a book priced at $3.99, you'll get a royalty of $2.99. (This is on Amazon, other sales platforms may vary). You'll need to sell a total of 16,723 books a year, 1,394 a month, and about 46 books a day. If you have five books out, you only need to sell 9 (16,723/5/365 = 9.2) of each title per day for a turnover of $50K.

Of course, you will have a multitude of products out once you've written your books, including Kindle copies, paperbacks, audio books, large print, and so on. You will also have costs involved in producing all of these products as well as advertising expenditure, but this example shows how having as many books published as possible helps you reach your goal of making a living with your writing. (See also examples in Chapter 3)

Recognize the fear you have inside . If you can't identify it, use methods like F-R-E-E-Writing to reveal your innermost thoughts. Analyse your fear and deal with it head on. The only way you deal with it is to ride it. Show that fearful person inside you that you are stronger than they think.

In the next chapter I talk about something that may be why you are not writing – writer's block.

5
WRITER'S BLOCK

What is writer's block and do you have it? Wikipedia defines the condition as:

Writer's block is a condition, primarily associated with writing, in which an author loses the ability to produce new work or experiences a creative slowdown. This loss of ability to write and produce new work is not a result of commitment problems or the lack of writing skills. The condition ranges from difficulty in coming up with original ideas to being unable to produce a work for years. Writer's block is not solely measured by time passing without writing. It is measured by time passing without productivity in the task at hand. (Wikipedia.org)

I've personally suffered from writer's block on a couple of occasions, and have found a few techniques to deal with it. Below are ones that worked well for me, ones that I have found through my research, and some that have been recommended by other writers.

Start another project

If you really cannot face your current project, write something else for a change. I tend to have several projects on the go at the same time, especially if I am starting a new book. Over time, say a week or two, I let the project in which I have the most interest take over. When I've finished with this project, I may go back to the other one, or I may leave it for another few months. Sometimes that book is never written. I have several unfinished novels in my virtual drawer, but I view these drafts as a little treasure trove. If I ever lack ideas, I go to these incomplete manuscripts to see if any of them piques my interest. I have yet to resume work on any of them, but you never know, one of these days I may.

The worst thing you can do is to carry on writing a story that bores you. If your manuscript bores you while you're writing it, can you imagine what a reader will make of it?

A word of warning, however. Exercise extreme caution when starting several projects at the same time. I know many new, and experienced, writers who have started two or three projects, and then cannot decide between them. This indecision blocks their writing, and they can't carry on with any of them. They end up totally blocked.

I fell into this category when I first started writing.

I had nearly finished the novel *Coffee and Vodka*, which was my MA in Creative Writing project. I also had an idea for a spy story, *The Red King of Helsinki,* which I began writing just after finishing my course but before completing the MA novel. On top of this, before fully finishing the spy thriller, I began blogging about the story behind my move to the UK, which eventually became *The English Heart*. To top it all, each of these manuscripts is in a different genre. *Coffee and Vodka* is literary fiction, *The Red King of Helsinki* a spy thriller, and *The English Heart* a romance. Writing in different genres can be a way to discover what you are best at, but it is time-consuming and can block your creativity. In my experience, either writing several projects at the same time, or/and creating books in different genres is quite typical for authors who are starting out. For me, writing in these different genres gave me experience of each and eventually a firm direction for my future writing.

I got out of this dilemma when I decided to self-publish. I needed a completed novel, so I finished *The English Heart first* and published it. The book was such a success that I decided to get the other two books out too. Later, I began writing a sequel to *The English Heart*, eventually writing six books in *The Nordic Heart* series.

I was motivated by the success of the three books. Until recently, *The English Heart* was by far the most successful of my books, although the other two continue to have steady monthly sales.

Two techniques

If you are in a rut because you can' decide between several projects, I would try two techniques.

The first one is to devote a week to each project.

If writing is simply out of the question, devote your time to research, or just read what you've written so far. Rate your interest level, either using the number of words you've managed to write in the week, or by giving your enthusiasm a score out of 10. Or both. Compare the results for each title and make your decision based on this. Don't forget, you can always come back to the other projects after you've finished (or published) the first one. At this stage, I would ignore any market conditions – which is the more popular genre, or which book would sell best. If your inability to choose between projects stops you from writing at all, it's best to write what interests you most. Readers can tell when a writer is bored. And boring your reader is the worst crime a writer can commit. And just getting any book out is better than not writing at all.

The second technique for overcoming paralysis when you can't decide between projects is to start a completely new book. The trick here is to stick with this new project. Mentally shackle yourself to your new manuscript. Forget about the plots, characters and the writing you've completed on the other projects. Tell yourself that you will come back to them when you've finished the new book. Naturally, this new project needs to keep you interested. If it becomes just another manuscript that you are mentally juggling, give it up, and try the first technique again.

At the end, you need to make a decision and stick to it. Did I say writing is easy?

Fiction and nonfiction

Many writers I know, me included, sometimes have a nonfiction title on the go at the same time as a novel. They alternate between the two, perhaps writing fiction in the morning and nonfiction in the afternoon. It's all about scheduling your day (see Chapter 3). Alternating between manuscripts can motivate you to write much more than you otherwise would.

For me, this phase doesn't last long, because the nonfiction loses out as I get more and more interested in the fiction. This is why, in order to get the nonfiction book finished, I set up a pre-order almost as soon as I start writing the manuscript. This sounds a bit like putting a gun to my own head, but I've found it is the only way I will ever finish a nonfiction book. You have to do what works for you.

Network

One way to get out of the rut of a writer's block is to go and see other people. Talking with other writers and creative people can be a good source of inspiration as well as commiseration.

When I was struggling to get on with *The True Heart,* the fourth book in *The Nordic Heart* series, I attended as many social events as I could. I was lucky that this was in November and December, when there were drinks parties galore. Even during the COVID pandemic, when gatherings are limited or not happening at all, you can take part in Zoom calls or online seminars.

When you connect with other authors, you may not want to talk about your block, but if you do, be honest. If you have the courage to admit to being blocked, you'll be amazed how many other writers will share their own stories with you. Some of them may be able to offer useful insights, especially if they know you well. One of my writing friends suggested that I might not be able to finish the book because I didn't want to say goodbye to the characters. *The True Heart* was supposed to be the last book in the series. (It wasn't, I wrote another one after that called *The Christmas Heart*). I hadn't thought of that.

Examine your emotions

Writing about characters you get to know intimately is a very emotional process. Examine your relationship with the book you are writing. Perhaps that's where your block is coming from?

For years I planned to write a mystery series set in the archipelago between Finland and Sweden. I felt the Åland Islands would be perfect for a Nordic Noir title, but I just couldn't get past 10,000 words. When I told a fellow writer about my idea, how I'd spent many summers on these islands, and how I loved their stark beauty and quirky island characters, she wondered if, deep down, I didn't want anything bad to happen in my summer paradise. How right she was! That was exactly why I was blocked. I decided to write a series of women's fiction titles set in the islands instead. This new series, *Love on the Island*, has become even more successful than *The English Heart*. All I needed was to forget about murder and mayhem and write about the characters' lives and loves instead!

Read

Reading novels and books in your own genre can be good preparation for writing. When you are blocked, this is even more critical. Even rereading a book that you admire, examining each scene, each plot point, and every character's journey and motivation, will give insights into how you can improve your own story. Similarly, if you are writing a nonfiction title, reading other books on the subject will give you ideas for your own title. I am not talking about plagiarism in either case, but reading other writers is never wasted time. That's how all writers learn.

Remember, writing is a craft.

Reading out of your genre, especially nonfiction, is also an excellent idea when you feel blocked. *The Artist's Way* by Julia Cameron, *The Chimp Paradox* by Professor Steve Peters, and *Productivity for Authors* by Joanna Penn are just a few books that I would recommend if you feel blocked.

Learn a new skill

Learning a new skill, whether it's chess, some form of exercise, a new language, or something to do with writing itself, such as learning to use a new piece of editing software, can give you a confidence boost and help you get over writer's block.

You could take a seminar on the business side of writing, as I did when I was blocked with *The True Heart*. During this excellent day, organized by Orna Ross and Joanna Penn, I realized I had a terrible relationship with money, and guessed this might be the root of my problems with writing – and with my confidence. To explore this relationship further, I read *You are a Badass at Making Money* by Jen Sincero. Wow, did this book make me think! I recommend you read it, even if you think you and money are all OK.

But it wasn't until I did a session on public speaking with speaker mentor Emma Stroud that something clicked. I'd always thought I was a pretty awful speaker, which was why I spent a lot of time practising beforehand – writing presentations well ahead of time, hiding behind Power Point images, and generally getting into a terrible state at book readings or public-speaking events. But during improvisation session with Emma, I suddenly realized I was actually quite good at talking on my feet. Who would have thought?

Both courses gave me confidence and spurred me on to finish *The True Heart*.

Research

When I was doing my MA in Creative Writing, one of my tutors recommended doing research when we were unable to write for whatever reason. My book *The Faithful Heart* is set in the 1990s, so I began researching the music, fashions, and news of the era. I had already done some of this, but walking through Soho in London I found a shop selling vintage women's magazines (now sadly closed) and bought a couple from 1990 and 1992. Leafing through the magazines, I got a possible idea for the plot.

Researching photo archives of the period, I came across a picture of the late Princess of Wales with one of my husband's captains. I got the idea of adding a Royal visit to the submarine on which my hero worked. More research led to a new and much more dramatic plot line.

You can research online from the comfort of your home, but it can be more inspiring to get out and visit libraries, art galleries and even travel to the setting of your story, if you have the time and can afford it. I'm writing this in London in the midst of the COVID pandemic, so research opportunities are limited, but when times return to normal, I recommend getting out there and seeing the world. Even if you haven't got any particular research in mind, just going to see an art exhibition or a play, or going for a walk in the forest or park, can bring surprising insights into your manuscript. Letting your mind rest for a while, or think about something completely different, can stimulate new ideas. If I had a pound for every time I think of a new character or plot twist while walking the dog, I'd be a millionaire.

All of these activities can take you out of your own life and situation and provide a new perspective on your work. In the next chapter I get into the nitty-gritty of training yourself to write every day: scheduling your writing time.

6
SCHEDULE YOUR WRITING TIME

The first step to making sure you create a sustainable writing routine is to create a schedule for your writing. This may sound simple, but scheduling your writing time is the most important thing you can do. I talk a lot in this book about writing every day (it is the title after all!), but I know a daily routine isn't for everyone. However, I argue, that even if your routine is to provide yourself with regular amounts of writing time, even if they are in bursts of a few days or a few weeks, this constitutes a sustainable writing routine. Especially, if you regularly produce a good amount of work this way.

In an interview for the *Paris Review*, the Nobel Prize-winning writer Doris Lessing said, 'When I was bringing up a child I taught myself to write in very short concentrated bursts. If I had a weekend, or a week, I'd do unbelievable amounts of work.' (https://www.theparisreview.org/interviews/2537/the-art-of-fiction-no-102-doris-lessing)

Doris Lessing wasn't a believer in writing every day, but she had a routine nevertheless, something she put down to habit, and became a prolific writer.

When can you write?

To begin the process of establishing a routine, ask yourself the question, 'When do I realistically have time to write? How can you carve time out from a busy lifestyle? You'd be surprised when you start looking at your day, how easy it is to find an hour, or two, for writing. First, identify your free time. What do you do with it at the moment? Do you watch TV, are you a keen gamer, do you meet up with friends or have a time-consuming hobby? Which of these could you give up or cut down on?

If you find yourself struggling with finding a time when you can write, think of the writing time as a meeting with someone very important who you cannot reschedule. Writing is your VIP, and the time you have allocated to it cannot be moved.

Let's say you have procured a time slot with a lifestyle guru of some sort. This person is in high demand but has offered you a set of month-long sessions, for which you pay through the nose. The guru could also be a financial adviser or a highly-sought after personal trainer. To take advantage of this wonderful opportunity to get rich, get fit, or get happy, you will do anything to make the sessions. Right?

The possibilities for finding time even in a busy day are endless. If you have a long commute to work, why not dedicate that time to writing? Or take your lunch hour in a café, where you can write on a laptop or other portable device. Or reduce your TV time in the evenings, or your meetings with friends. If you are serious about writing, finding time is your priority.

Perhaps time itself is not the issue. Many of the writers I help in my consultancy start writing when they reach retirement, or when their children start school or leave home for university, or if their job situation has changed. However, even when time is plentiful, it can still be difficult to get down to writing, so it is very important to define a time when you are going to do nothing but write.

Once you have identified a time, preferably every day, when you are going to write, remember to treat writing as if it is a crucial business meeting that you cannot miss.

My routine

My writing routine is something that many authors share. I have allocated mornings to writing, mainly because my brain is sharper at that time of the day. As a full-time writer, I also need to look after the production of my books, and the marketing and PR. This involves everything from working with editors, proofreaders, cover designers, and marketing professionals. I look after my own advertising and book pricing, as well as run my own email subscription list. I write a newsletter once a week, run promotional campaigns, outline my own book launches, and run a book publishing and marketing consultancy on the side. So you can see, as a self-published author, there is always something else, apart from writing, that I could be doing. But I keep my mornings free for writing, ensuring I complete my daily word count, because it is what I do. I am a writer. When I gave up full-time work, I used to have that sentence, I AM A WRITER, pinned to the wall above my computer. It would remind me that I had to write every day, whatever else happened.

Form a habit of writing

As well as deciding on a regular time for writing, take some time to decide where you are going to write. Humans are creatures of habit. According to a 2012 study by the *British Journal of General Practice* it can take between 18 and 255 days to form a habit, depending on what kind of habit. Humans create habits because they are easy for our brains. (https://www.ncbi.nlm.nih.gov/pmc/articles/PMC3505409/)

The above study was commissioned to help patients form healthy habits that would ensure a longer and healthier life. But these recommendations can just as easily be adopted for creating a sustainable writing routine.

1. Decide on a goal you want to achieve with your writing routine.
2. Choose a simple action that will get you towards your goal, which you can do on a daily basis.
3. Plan when and where you will do your chosen action. Be consistent: choose a time and place that you encounter every day of the week.
4. Every time you encounter that time and place, do the action.
5. It will get easier with time. Within 10 weeks you should find you are doing it automatically without even having to think about it.
6. Congratulations, you've created a sustainable writing routine!

The above may seem simplistic to you, but believe me, it works.

Point one in the action plan is about setting targets, which I will deal with in the next chapter. Point two deals with scheduling your writing, which I have already discussed, but it also concerns the space in which you choose to write. Ensure that the spot is just for writing. It can be the same place where you do other things, but make sure you remove all unnecessary reminders of the other things you do with the computer, or at the same desk. If you have somewhere at home where your writing space it set out – whether it is in the corner of the living room, in the kitchen or in a dedicated office – put away any physical files from your desk, close down your email programme, and remove any other pop-ups you have. If you are able to take a lunch hour in the office, try to find somewhere other than your usual desk to do your writing and make sure everyone knows you are not to be disturbed.

Many writers find a place outside of home or office to write. Whether it's a café, a library or a co-working space, try to ensure you can write at the same desk or table every time. This makes it easier for you to concentrate and the words will come more easily during your allocated writing time.

Even if you can work from home, you may not be able to concentrate because of other demands on your time, be it washing, cleaning or whatever small talk your brain invents to distract you from writing.

It's been said that writers are the world's masters at inventing displacement activities. It's amazing, for example, how well my houseplants have done since I gave up my office job and began my full-time career as a writer. I hate cleaning and ironing, but I can spend a stupidly long time taking care of my pot plants, on the balcony and inside. I tell myself this provides invaluable thinking time before I settle down to type, but I know (and now you know too) that this is a barefaced lie! Still, my plants thrive.

But, and this is an important but, I do eventually get down to writing. Pottering about with my plants has now become part of my routine, which is important in forming a writing habit. So do take point three in the above schedule seriously. It is the simple routines – indicators that tell your brain you are going to write – that work. Perhaps you make yourself a cup of coffee, give your desk a quick tidy up, or put on your comfortable 'writing' pants.

Forming a routine for writing is hugely important. If you are in the same space and do the same things every time you begin writing, your brain will understand that this is the time for you to produce some great words. This is why it's so important to allocate a time – and a place for your writing.

Remember writing is your job. If you want to be a successful writer, you need to write. The idea that a writer – or any artist – has to wait for the magical muse to visit in order to produce great works is highly misleading. I do believe that the concept of the muse, or the artist's inspiration, that originated in Greek mythology has its place in modern life, but I believe that you can invoke this 'higher spirit of inspiration' by forming a habit of writing. You'll find that the more often you sit down at your writing desk, the more often the writer's muse visits.

As the American writer and activist Mary Heaton Vorse said to Sinclair Lewis (who later won the Nobel Prize for Literature), 'The art of writing is the art of applying the seat of the pants to the seat of the chair.' (https://quoteinvestigator.com/2015/09/24/chair/)

So apply the seat of your pants to the seat of your writing chair every day, and eventually, I guarantee, inspiration will strike.

Get help

If you already have a few books published and struggle to find time from all the other tasks a writer has to do, get yourself some help. This kind of investment may seem foolhardy, especially at the beginning of a writing career, but as you see from the example on page xxx, every book that you publish should bring you more income.

There are many online tools that you can use to minimize the time you spend at certain tasks, such as social media posts, managing your email list, and book marketing.

I use MeetEdgar to schedule my social media posts and to recycle my blog posts both from my Selfpublishingcoach.co.uk and helenahalme.com sites. I also use TweetDeck to schedule Twitter posts, especially if I have a book promotion on, or if I'm launching a new book.

I use Mailchimp and BookFunnel to manage my email list, and Vellum to format the interior files of my books into both eBooks and paperbacks.

To employ of a Virtual Assistant (VA) is something I have on my wish list, and I am currently looking for someone to manage my two websites.

In order to increase your productivity and give yourself as much writing time as possible, it's good to start from what you are currently doing. Set out all the tasks you complete in a day and a week, and see which function could be taken over by a piece of software, another site, or an assistant.

When you are starting out, it's difficult to see how you could spend any money on outside help, but it's worth making the investment if it means you are able to publish books more frequently. Naturally, you have to be careful to make sure you don't overextend yourself. But once you have a few books out, it's really worth examining where your time goes and whether it is time spent productively, or if something or someone else could do it for you.

In the next chapter I will go more deeply into how you can make yourself write every day with setting your targets.

7

SET TARGETS

In the previous chapter, we talked about the reasons why you may not be writing. In this chapter, I will take you through one of the main ways you can motivate yourself to write every day: setting targets.

Word count

One of the most important targets you need to set is a word count for the day, week and month. Every writer has an optimum number of words they can write each day. It depends on experience, on the type of book, and on the kind of writer. Some authors aim to write perfect text, while others are more interested in putting down ideas, and correcting the work later. It's worth noting again that the first draft is never perfect. Every writer's work is edited, corrected and proofread.

The word count you can achieve also depends on what you are writing. Below is a rough guide to the word count of various types of books:

- Short story: under 7,500
- Novella: 17,500– 40,000
- Novel: 40,000– 90,000
- Nonfiction: 20,000+

The definition of a book changes all the time. We are living in a fast, digital world, which means that short reads are increasingly popular. A few years ago, Amazon introduced categories for 'Kindle Short Reads', listing books according to the time it takes an average reader to finish them, rather than their page counts. Here are the categories of Kindle Shorts:

- 15 minutes (1–11 pages)
- 30 minutes (12–21 pages)
- 45 minutes (22–32 pages)
- 1 hour (33–43 pages)
- 90 minutes (44–64 pages)
- 2 hours or more (65–100 pages)

Taking into account that an average page is 250–300 words, a 15-minute read is therefore 4,500 words. As I write this, the US Amazon Kindle Short Reads category is dominated by comedian and actor Mindy Kaling, whose essays are around 20 pages each (6,000 words). All five of her books were published simultaneously in October 2020. The No.1 in the category deals with her Indian heritage and is currently estimated by Publisher Rocket (https://publisherrocket.com) to be selling around 87,000 copies a month. Priced at $1.99, these short books are, according to my calculations, earning Mindy Kaling and her publisher (Amazon) a million dollars each month.

If we assume Ms Kaling writes every day and produces 1,000 words per session, it took her just

60 days – or two months – to produce the first draft for these ten 'Kindle Shorts'. Allowing for a similar time for editing, plus some time for formatting and the cover designs, the whole project took about 6-8 months. Pretty good for a monthly turnover of 1 million dollars?

We can't all be famous comedians with a multi-million dollar publishing and retail giant behind us, but Mindy Kaling proves what can be done with a daily writing routine and fast publishing.

Once you've decided on the type of book you are going to write, set targets. Don't forget, if you want to follow in Mindy Kaling's steps, you need to publish your short reads either simultaneously, or in very quick succession, so it's best to have them ready at the same time. I know many indie writers who have written three to five novellas, or short reads, and published them in monthly chunks for readers to enjoy – very much as Dickens did when he published *Pickwick Papers* nearly two hundred years ago.

You can set your targets on an Excel spreadsheet, note them down in a diary, or even on a black-board in your office. Whichever way you choose, make sure you can easily update them and enjoy the sense of satisfaction you get when you achieve your daily goal. I am a novelist, so I write long form. I add my target words to a tab on the document I use to chart the plot and the characters of the book.

The benefits of setting a daily word goal are many.

Firstly, you will be able to plan when your launch should be. You can book editors, the cover and layout designers, and even plan advertising for the launch. You can start 'warming up' your audience, whether on social media or through your email list. You can tease your readers with snippets of your writing or give them an exclusive cover reveal.

The word count also introduces accountability to your writing routine. Treat the spread sheet, or whatever you use for your target word count, as if it was your agent or publisher. You've promised them a finished manuscript on a certain day, and if you can't make that day, you have to have a very good excuse for being late.

You can also use your word count spread sheet to

timetable your own edits and those of your editor, proofreading, and launch dates for the eBook and paperback.

Overleaf is an example of a word count plan for one of my recent books.

WORD COUNT SCHEDULE

The Island Daughter

DATE	WORDS BALANCE	WORDS DAY	TARGET WORDS	TARGET BALANCE	VARIANCE
21/02/20	2,000	2,000	1,500	1,500	500
22/02/20	3,000	1,000	1,500	3,000	0
23/02/20	5,500	2,500	1,500	4,500	1,000
24/02/20	8,500	3,000	1,500	6,000	2,500
25/02/20	10,950	2,450	1,500	7,500	3,450
26/02/20	11,450	500	1,500	9,000	2,450
27/02/20	11,950	500	1,500	10,500	1,450
28/02/20	12,950	1,000	1,500	12,000	950
29/02/20	14,950	2,000	1,500	13,500	1,450
01/03/20	15,450	500	1,500	15,000	450

DATE	WORDS BALANCE	WORDS DAY	TARGET WORDS	TARGET BALANCE	VARIANCE
22/05/20	67,490	500	1,500	67,500	-10
23/05/20	67,990	500	1,500	69,000	-1,010
24/05/20	70,990	3,000	1,500	70,500	490
25/05/20	73,990	3,000	1,500	72,000	1,990
26/05/20	73,990	0	1,500	73,500	490
27/05/20	**Pre-order live**		Self Edit		
30/05/20			1st Reader		
03/06/20			**Send ARCs**		
04/06/20			Launch Crew Read		
12/06/20			**ARC Deadline**		
13/06/20			Self Edit		
14/06/20			To Editor		
15/06/20			Editor		
28/06/20			Self Edit		
29/06/20			Order PB proof		
30/06/20			Editor 2nd pass		
08/07/20			Self Edit		
10/07/20			Proofreader		
13/07/20			**Final Kindle upload**		
14/07/20			Proofread PB		
16/07/20			Final PB upload		
17/07/20			**PUBLICATION DAY**		

How many words a day

Every writer varies in how many words they can write each day. My target is at least 1,000 words per session, but often I get 2,000 words down every morning. If I'm having a bad day, I can allow myself just 500 words, but those days are getting few and far between.

Every writer is different, and certainly the more experienced you become, the more your daily word count increases. You also become more used to plotting your novel or planning the chapters in your nonfiction book, which increases the speed of your writing. The more you write, the better you become at the craft of writing. You are less likely to spend time searching for the right word, and you become more skilled at writing dialogue, building character and describing landscapes and scenes of any kind.

Don't set unachievable goals

When setting your daily word goal, don't forget that you do need to fulfil the targets you've set. I know this may sound silly, but I have often fallen into the trap of making fantastical plans, only to tumble at the first hurdle when I couldn't fulfil these ambitions. Success comes when we recognize our own abilities – and limitations. So set achievable targets. Remember that these are personal to you – only you will know if you can write 100, 500 or 10,000 words a day. How many words you manage each day is hugely individual. While you'll notice that your speed increases the more you write, don't try to write too much in a day. Working too intensely one day can often have consequences for the following day or days.

I have learned to temper my ambitions. It may seem ridiculous, especially if you are new to writing, but I try not to write too much in a day. If I have a whole day, when all I have to do is write, I can get up to 10,000 words. But the next day I am completely empty. I can hardly add 100 words to the manuscript. For me, personally – and, again, I can't stress enough how individual this is – my 'sweet spot' lies somewhere between 1,000 and 2,000 words. If I notice that I am going over 3,000 words, I stop, knowing that it will impact my creative energy for the next day or days.

It's also wise to set targets lower than you think your word count should be. If you think you could write 1,000 words a day, set your daily goal at, say, 750. It's hugely satisfying to have met the target at the end of the day, and it will give you an upbeat start to the next day's writing marathon. When you know you are ahead of the game, you tend to do better. There is nothing more depressing and demotivating than having to start the day with a negative balance.

New writers

If you are just starting out and don't have any idea how many words you are able to produce, start with a target of 500 words. Many authors, even quite well-known ones, have this as their daily goal. If your plan is to write, say a novel of roughly 70,000 words, you could get to a first draft manuscript in 140 days. That's just over four and a half months. With this kind of pace – writing every day – you could easily produce two books a year. You can see from my word count schedule that it takes about a month and a half for me to get from the first draft to the published novel. Together with the first draft writing time of four and a half months, this means six months in total.

Wouldn't you love to publish two books a year? With 500 words a day, this is entirely possible. Just think how many titles you could publish if you doubled that daily writing goal.

In the next few chapters, I'll talk more about how you can make writing every day easier, and slowly, with time and experience, increase your word count. First, I want to talk about the importance of plotting.

8

PLOT OR NOT TO PLOT?

If you write every day, it is easier to keep the story in your head, and you can twist and turn the story exactly as you like, without having to go back and remind yourself of the characters or plot so far. But the writing process is helped if you have a draft plot in place before you start.

Are you a plotter or a pantser?

In the writing community there is a never-ending debate over which is better, plotting a story before you begin writing, or making it up as you go along. Writers are categorized as plotters or pantsers. The first term is for writers like me, who like to plot before they write a single word, while the other one signifies someone who prefers to write by the seat of their pants without any fore-thought or planning.

Before I began writing every day, I was a mixture of both. But boy, was that hard. I've already mentioned how difficult it was coming back to a manuscript that had been left for days, weeks, or even months. Doing that without having any kind of plot, without the first idea of who your charac-ters are, is incredibly difficult. No wonder it took me years to write my first book!

Nowadays, I start the writing process with an idea. Sometimes the idea is just a character and a place I want to write about, sometimes it's based on a piece of news I've caught, or a moral dilemma I want to examine. Next, I see if I can turn the idea into a plot.

The story arc

I plot a story before I write even a single word, using the story arc method. This ensures that before I start writing, I know the bare bones of the outline of my story. So first, before I put down any words, I create a document that sets out the

the main plot points of the story arc. Below is a very simple image of the story arc concept.

- Inciting Incident
- Progressive Complications
- Crisis
- Climax
- Resolution

Each of my main characters has their own story arc. In a separate document I outline the various characters' likes, dislikes, internal fears, hates and loves. I list my characters' outward appearance as well as their motivations, both external and internal. During the writing process, I visit the document frequently, for inspiration and to check I'm keeping within the outlined plot.

Inciting incident

Every story starts with an inciting incident, which forces the main character(s) into action. In a romance, this is usually when the two lovers first meet, while in a crime thriller it's often the discovery of a body.

Progressive complications

Next, there are several progressive complications. The object of our protagonist's love finds out he has an incredible job offer on the other side of the world, but our protagonist doesn't want to leave her job behind. Or, while our detective investigates the murder, another body is found. These complications should get more serious as the story develops. In our crime thriller, for example, the detective finds himself in mortal danger as he gets closer to the perpetrator. Or, our lovers have continued their relationship through frequent Skype or Zoom calls, but it seems one of them is cheating, and there is a suspicion that this is not new.

Crisis

Inevitably, there is a crisis. The lovers have a huge fight, and break up, causing terrible heartache. Or our detective is held at gunpoint, all hope of rescue gone.

Climax

The climax sees the lovers make up. The suspected affair didn't exist, and the lovers reunite on the other side of the world. The detective cleverly overcomes his nemesis, or is rescued at the last minute by his fellow police officers – or even by a love interest.

Resolution

The resolution is where we find out who the murderer is, and why he carried out the murders. We see the detective musing over his clever detection, and getting back to his (often chaotic) life. The lovers are happy and planning their future together.

The resolution in a novel is a very important part of the story. It is the payback for the reader and should not be left out. Even though you could say the story ends in the climax, it's very important to give the reader an image of how the characters' life carries on. The readers have grown to love (or sometimes hate) the people in the book, so they need to have the satisfaction of seeing how they have survived the dramatic episode in their lives.

The benefits of plotting

It *is* possible to write successfully without any plotting whatsoever, and some authors are very successful in writing this way, but I would not recommend it.

Having a plot will inspire you to write every day. It will also give your writing a structure. Even if you don't write sequentially, from Chapter One to The End (and very few of us do!), having the bare bones of an outline will allow you to hop from one scene to another without getting into a muddle.

Not having a plot of any kind will significantly slow down your writing. I know it's difficult to take the time to plan ahead when all you want to do is write, but believe me, the days you take to plan and plot will reap huge benefits later on. And you can count this plotting time as writing time – just like you can the time you are editing.

Don't look at plotting as some boring pre-writing chore, like something you had to do at school or college. Look at it as the most exciting kind of brainstorming. This is the time when you can imagine worlds and scenarios for your characters. You can ask 'what if' questions galore, putting your characters in the most incredible situations and then getting them out in the nick of time. If you feel you want to write a scene while plotting, go ahead. This is what often happens to me – I am charting the course of the story and suddenly I can see it in front of me and what happens next, and I just have to write out the new scene. Naturally, this is easier when you have the rough outline of the story set out as shown in the previous paragraph, but there is nothing to stop you from going ahead with it straightaway. As long as you come back and finish the outline afterwards.

The hugely successful indie writer, K.M. Weiland, says in her new book, *Writing Your Story's Theme*, that she thinks the division between plotters and pantsers doesn't really exist. She thinks everybody has to plot at some point, the only difference is when you decide to do it – before writing or once you've written the first draft. (https://www.

thecreativepenn.com/2020/10/05/outlining-your-novel/)

Joanna Penn of The Creative Penn (https://www.thecreativepenn.com) talks about 'discovery writing', or finding the story through writing it. I think most of us are so-called discovery writers, even those who have a tight plot and a set of deeply thought-out characterizations. Something you hadn't planned always happens on the page. But, if you have really thought about the story in advance, it's easier to slot the new scene or plot twist into the story.

9

SMALL TIPS AND TRICKS

Once you've scheduled your writing time, examined why you are not writing, and set your targets, it's time to write. Making writing a daily habit is easier than you think. It may sound simple, but all you have to do is sit at your desk, open whichever application you use, and write. The words or sentences do not have to be perfect. You will have plenty of time to edit them, but you cannot edit an empty page. If you sit there long enough, I guarantee that inspiration will come. Especially if you have done all you can to set your brain on the right track.

In this chapter I want to give you some tips and tricks you can use to establish a sustainable writing routine.

Limit distractions

Limiting distractions is one of the most obvious ways to get into writing, but it's something many of us ignore. You may not even realize that something around you is stopping your flow of thoughts and making it more difficult for you to get the words down. Turning off social media, other windows and apps on your computer, and wearing noise-cancelling headphones may do the trick. We all have notifications popping up all the time on our screen, so turning them off is a good idea. There are many apps and programmes that can do this for you.

I used to think I could write anywhere, and to a certain extent this is true. I've done some of my best work on trains and airplanes, but this year, when my husband started to work from home, his voice from the next room really disturbed me. (He is constantly either on the phone, on a Zoom conference, or hosting a webinar). Eventually, I remembered that he had a pair of noise-cancelling headphones that he used when commuting on the London Underground. I began to use them when writing and it made a huge difference. Putting the headphones on is now part of my writing routine, integral to getting into the writing zone.

You may have some music that inspires you while you write, so put this on and add it to your writing routine.

Set a time limit

If you have a larger window for your writing session – say the whole morning – try setting smaller time limits within this period. I often do this when I need to fool myself into writing (see below). I say to myself, 'I'm going to write for the next half an hour and see how it goes. If nothing happens, I'll make another coffee.' Surprise, surprise, this never fails, and I find myself still tapping away two or three hours later. Making yourself sit at your desk, with just the writing software and your manuscript open in front of you, will eventually make you do something.

Leave a hook in your story

Another great method that many writers (including me) use is to leave a scene open when finishing a session. This acts as a hook for yourself, rather than your reader. (Although, if it is a hook that works, you might want to keep it.) I do this almost every time I write. If I'm in the middle of an exciting scene, and my word count is over my target for the day, I just stop. I know that the next day, writing will be easier because I will be starting from a very exciting point.

Alternatively, you could just write a few words of a new scene. I often write a brief two-sentence summary of a new section, knowing that this will make writing a hundred times easier the next day. Knowing what works for you is vital for establishing a sustainable writing routine.

Try not to edit

One of the easiest way to start your writing session is to read what you wrote during the last session. However, this method is full of pitfalls, because the first thing you start to do is edit the previous day's (or even week's) writing. Editing your own work is a vital part of the writing process, but it's best done in a structured way – after you've finished the first draft.

Of course, it's only natural to want to review your work before you begin writing again, especially if you haven't left a 'hook' for yourself. But it's important to control the desire to rewrite parts or even the whole manuscript. There is plenty of time to do that when your first draft is done.

One of my tutors on my MA in Creative Writing course recommended reading just 300 words of the previous day's writing for inspiration. I think this is good advice on the whole, but for me it's a little too prescriptive. Why not 500 words? A thousand? If I do start reading what I've written before, I will probably jump straight into editing mode.

If you have your characters and plot worked out, and you write regularly (hopefully every day), remembering where you were and what comes next – or what you want to write next – will come naturally to you. You should not need to read (and be tempted to edit) the work you've already done.

Don't get me wrong, editing your own work is vital, but if you start editing a manuscript that is not finished, you will not get any writing done. What's more, you may have to re-edit the passages again if the plot changes or you decide to add or leave out characters. It's best to leave the first draft imperfect and just get the words down. When you are more experienced, you'll find that the first version of your story will need less and less editing anyway.

Stay excited

Another of my tutors told me that the worst crime an author can commit is to bore the reader. And how do we know if we are boring the reader when everyone's tastes are different? By not boring ourselves when writing the story.

If you find yourself in a dull part of your manuscript, but think you have to write out, stop. Just stop writing and go to a scene you find exciting. If you are bored by your own narrative, just imagine how the reader will feel. You may find that you won't need that scene or chapter. The 'boring' information may slot into another scene, if it is needed at all. When you start writing, make sure you are always excited about the words you are setting down. This ensures that you'll never bore the reader, and you will keep yourself motivated.

Another way to keep yourself excited and engaged with the story is to commission the cover design. To me, this phase is always exciting. I try to have the jacket done as soon as I know how the story is going to pan out.

Turn off your inner critic

This is a difficult one, but essential if you are to write every day and finish that manuscript.

At the beginning of this book I said how writing and publishing quickly, without considering the quality of the writing, isn't enough to ensure success. The books you publish have to be very good, even excellent, for you to be successful. This is a hugely important point, but one that you shouldn't dwell on while writing the first draft.

I don't believe anyone, including masters such as Dickens and Shakespeare, would have written a word had they not believed in themselves and turned off their inner critic while they wrote.

Hemingway (or possibly someone else) said, 'The first draft of anything is shit.' And he was right. Nobody, nobody publishes their first draft. First drafts are there to be corrected and edited. They are merely a statement of ideas, a rough course of events for your story. It's only in the editing process that the gem that is a very good, or excellent, story emerges. In the beginning of my career I lost count of how many edits I made to my first manuscripts. The editing phase is as important, if not more critical, than the writing phase. But – and this is an important but – you cannot edit an empty page.

You have to believe in yourself as a writer, in your story and in your ability to edit the work after you've finished the first draft. With each manuscript and book, you will become a better writer. Writing is a craft. You WILL improve.

Get an accountability partner

It's much easier to reach targets if you've told someone about your plans. Having another person with whom you can share your progress can be a huge motivational resource. This accountability partner can be anyone. It can be your partner, a member of your family or a friend, another writer, or even someone completely different. As long as this person understands the creative process and is supportive, you will find that their presence in your corner will help you reach your word target.

My accountability partner is my husband. He doesn't really know he is, but I've noticed, especially during the COVID lockdowns, that I write a lot more when he's around! We both work from home nowadays. At first, I found it difficult to ignore him in the room next to me; now his presence makes me work harder. I tell him about my writing and publishing plans over lunch, and he tells me about his day so far. I love it when I can tell him that I've exceeded my target word count for the morning.

Set a pre-order

Another way to motivate yourself to write is to set the book for pre-order. You can do this without having to upload the manuscript on both Amazon

KDP and Apple, as long as you have a cover ready.

This is the most effective way to motivate myself to write every day. It's a high-risk strategy, because platforms such as Amazon KDP allow you to postpone the publication date only once before applying penalties. At the moment, a second postponement will incur a twelve-month ban on setting pre-orders. Naturally, it's not good for your image either. Readers who've already pre-ordered the title, will be notified of the change. They will be disappointed, and may cancel their order. Many a time have I cursed myself for boldly setting a title out for pre-order! But I've only changed the date on a couple of occasions, and each time for a very good reason. Because, my dear fellow writers, whatever plans you make, sometimes life just happens.

Don't be too hard on yourself if you have to postpone publication. Next time, set the date further down the road.

Fool yourself into writing

I find that the most difficult stage of writing every day is the start. Let me explain. For me at least, and I have heard this from many other authors, some mornings I don't even want to open Scrivener, the software I use for all my writing. To overcome this, I fool myself into writing. I tell myself that I will try to write for a few minutes, and if nothing comes, I'll give up. I very rarely do. Almost every time, I'm still sitting at my desk an hour or two later. Every day, I write my target words and more. Of course, I use every trick that I have included in this book: I plot in advance, I set my target words, I have a space where I always write and a routine, I have my accountability partner, and I set the book out for pre-order a lot sooner than I should. I have a very regular daily routine with exercise and set mealtimes. All of this helps to ensure that I use my time efficiently, almost as if I was working in an office. Sometimes I think I work at least 50% more efficiently than I did when I was office based, but this is difficult to measure as I've never worked as a writer in an office.

When I was working in an office, and writing was my second job, I saw writing as a reward. It took me a long time to get past this notion. For a long time after I'd begun writing full-time, I'd do everything that I found boring, like marketing or social media (I love some of it, but not all), before allowing myself to write. It took me months to realize what the issue was. It was only when I did NaNoWriMo that I finally understood that writing is my job, and the most important part of being a self-published author is to write every day. All the other tasks are secondary.

I talked in Chapter 4 about identifying the reason why you aren't writing, and this is critical to getting into a daily routine. For me, it was the silly notion that writing was a reward, but it may be something else for you.

Set triggers

In Chapter 6, where I talked about forming a habit, I mentioned how important it is to give the brain clues that this is your writing time. My daily routine starts with breakfast, during which I read my emails, check the diary for the day's appointments, and look at the previous night's sales. I potter about with my plants for a while, then make a second coffee and take it into my study. Those are my preparations for writing. If you can't always write in the same place, try to adopt other rituals. If you're using software to block notices or the web browser, setting these up may do the trick. If you write in a café, just entering the place, ordering your drink and sitting down will tell your brain that this is your writing time.

It's best to write in the mornings, if you can. Your brain is fresh, so you will produce more words and better words. Waking up an hour or two before you usually do is a method many writers use. I don't do that anymore, but I did when I did my first NaNoWrimo (see Chapter 1). I woke up at 5.30 and wrote my 1,600 words before breakfast.

Now, if I haven't written anything in a day, I feel jittery. My daily writing routine is part of who I am.

Reward yourself

While it's good to be disciplined and best to keep the target fairly low, so that it's easy to exceed it, it is also important to reward yourself. This is one of the most important little tips that I have for you.

Give yourself a target for the next hour, such as reaching a certain number of words, or finishing a scene or a chapter. When you've reached your goal, give yourself a coffee, go for a walk, or even spend some time internet browsing. It may just be spending a few moments on a favourite site, listening to some music, reading a book, whatever. But make sure it's something that will leave you feeling good about yourself, and something that you can do every day. This little reward will also become a part of your routine and will segue nicely into your other tasks of the day.

10

TAKE CARE

I've talked a lot about the benefits of writing every day. However, you must also take care of yourself. Writing is an intense activity, and it is important that you don't overdo it.

Burnout

Recently, there have been reports of self-published authors experiencing burnout. Many of us push ourselves to the limit. Our work is demanding, especially if we are ambitious. Creating vivid, engaging, and coherent text isn't easy. Using our imaginations every day to invent a new world, new characters and plot lines takes a toll on our whole beings.

If you feel tired and grumpy all the time, if writing seems like a chore, and if none of my tips and tricks in this book help, you might have burnout.

To avoid it, be sure to take breaks from writing and don't overdo it. Listen to your body, and do only as much as is safe for you. As I mentioned before, I've learned from experience not to write too many words each day.

You can use any of the tips and tricks set out in Chapter 5 on writer's block (which can also be caused by burnout) or take a day, a week, or even a month off and do whatever else you like. If you set a time for how long you are going to be away from writing, you won't feel guilty. Writers write about the world and life, so sometimes you need to live it a little too.

Breathing time

Don't forget that editing and re-writing time is also 'writing time'. You can see from my Word Count Schedule in Chapter 7 that I do not have any target words for the days when the manuscript is with my first reader, editor, advance readers or proof reader. It's great if you can use this free time to start plotting a new story, or even writing one. I've tried this many times with varying degrees of success. If the next book is in a series, I may write a few scenes, just to make it easier for me to start the book in earnest when the current one is published. However, I often fail in this task and end up feeling frustrated and disappointed in myself. As a result, I now allow myself some breathing time between projects. There is always a lot of marketing tasks for a new book, so I focus on those and begin my daily writing routine again when I start editing (or rewriting) the manuscript according to comments I've received from either my readers or editor.

Celebrate

When your book is published, it's time to celebrate. Have a holiday or a break from writing for a week or two. Enjoy watching the increased sales a new book brings and let your mind rest.

However, it's very easy to fall into a trap at this stage. The sense of achievement after publication is dizzying, but the most important thing you can do now is to start a new project. Remember the chart in Chapter 3? The more you publish the more successful you'll be. So it's important to get back to your daily writing routine. If your mind feels empty, and you really do not know what to write next, examine the reasons you aren't writing by using the methods described in Chapter 5. Often, acknowledging the reasons for your lack of enthusiasm is enough to solve the problem and get you back to your routine. Or try some of the techniques described in Chapter 5 to overcome writer's block. You'll probably just need a little inspiration.

If I've been able to take time off after publication, I usually find I have too many ideas for the next book. I have been writing a series set on the Scandinavian Åland Islands for a couple of years now, which makes deciding what to write next a little easier. Often, I don't have space for all the plot lines in one novel, so they spill into the next one, giving me a 'free' start on the story.

Or you could have a look at the projects you abandoned before writing the book you have just published. Are you still interested in any of those stories? Could they be made more engaging for you and your readers? This is the time to play around with ideas, have brainstorming sessions. This is the fun part, so don't rush it. You've written and published a book before, you can do it again!

OVER TO YOU

I hope I've shown you how you can motivate yourself to write every day for success. Through the ten steps I've outlined above, I'm certain you'll be able to establish a sustainable writing habit.

Don't forget to be honest with yourself if you aren't writing. Think hard and use the techniques I've outlined to find out why. If you're afraid that you're not good enough, know that this is how most writers sometimes feel. If you want to be a writer, at some point you do have to write. If you establish a good, sustainable writing routine, you will reach this dream a lot sooner than if you wait for inspiration.

Writing every day will make it easier to stay motivated. It will feed your creativity and enable you to see the whole project more clearly. It will make you into a writer.

Write every day but don't forget to be good to yourself at the same time. And don't forget to let me know how you're getting on!

ACKNOWLEDGMENTS

As usual, I couldn't have completed this book without the constant encouragement of my husband and first reader, David Frise.

I'd also like to thank my coaching clients, especially Freddie P. Peters, why soured me on to Strat this title in the first instance. Her enthusiasm for my work makes me often wonder who the coach and who the client is.

My editor, Dorothy Stannard, (with the patience of a saint) turned this manuscript around in record time. I promise one of these days I will not rush you!

Thanks must also go to Orna Ross of the Alliance of Independent Authors and Joanna Penn of the Creative Penn for their constant inspiration and support.

A NOTE FROM THE AUTHOR

I would greatly appreciate it if you could write a short review of this book on Amazon.

Thank you.

WRITE YOUR STORY
TURN YOUR LIFE INTO FICTION IN 10 EASY STEPS

Do you want to write your own life story but don't know how to turn real events into fiction?

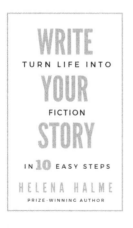

"Short how-to that inspired the writer hidden within!"

Write Your Story **is now available in good book-shops and online.**

WRITE IN ANOTHER LANGUAGE
10 EASY STEPS

In *Write in Another Language* I share with you a few practical tips on how to write in a language that is not your mother tongue.

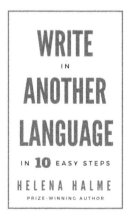

"Helena's experience and tips are excellent."

Write in Another Language is now available in good bookshops and online.

ABOUT THE AUTHOR

Helena Halme grew up in Tampere, Finland, and moved to the UK via Stockholm and Helsinki in her twenties. She's a former BBC journalist, magazine editor, and bookseller.

Since gaining an MA in Creative Writing at Bath Spa University, Helena has published two nonfiction and nine fiction titles, including three in *Love on the Island* series.

Helena lives in North London with her ex-Navy husband. She loves Nordic Noir and sings along to Abba songs when no-one is listening.

You can read Helena's blog selfpublishingcoach.
co.uk where you can also sign up for her self-
publishing tips.

ALSO BY HELENA HALME

Nonfiction

Write Your Story: Turn Your Life into Fiction in Ten
Easy Steps

Write in Another Language: Ten Easy Steps

Write Every Day: Motivate Yourself to Success in Ten
Easy Steps

Fiction

The Nordic Heart Series:

The Young Heart (Prequel)

The English Heart (Book 1)

The Faithful Heart (Book 2)

The Good Heart (Book 3)

The True Heart (Book 4)

The Christmas Heart (Book 5)

The Nordic Heart Boxset Books 1-4

Love on the Island Series:

The Day We Met: Prequel Short Story

The Island Affair (Book 1)

An Island Christmas (Book 2)

The Island Daughter (Book 3)

An Island Summer (Book 4 – out spring 2021)

Love on the Island Boxset Books 1-3

<u>Other titels:</u>

Coffee and Vodka: A Nordic family drama

The Red King of Helsinki: Lies, Spies and Gymnastics

Printed in Great Britain
by Amazon

56725348R00068